TRUST BASED LEADERSHIP

Proven Ways to Stop Managing and Start Leading

MARK GIVEN
Founder of the Trust Based Philosophy™

Copyright © 2018 Mark Given

ALL RIGHT RESERVED. No part of this book or its associated ancillary materials may be reproduced or transmitted in any form or by any means, electronic or mechanical, including photocopying, recording, or by any informational storage or retrieval system without permission from the publisher.

For publishing consideration:
markgivenseminars@gmail.com

ISBN: 978-1-7320146-0-2

DISCLAIMER AND/OR LEGAL NOTICES
While all attempts have been made to verify information provided in this book and its ancillary materials, neither the author nor publisher assumes any responsibility for errors, inaccuracies or omissions and is not responsible for any financial loss by customers in any manners. Any slights of people or organizations are unintentional. If advice concerning legal, financial, accounting or related matters in needed, the services of a qualified professional should be sought. This book and its associated ancillary materials, including verbal and written training, in not intended for use as a source of legal, financial or accounting advice. You should be aware of the various laws governing business transactions or other business practices in your particular geographic location.

The author has made every effort to ensure the accuracy of the information within this book was correct at time of publication. The author does not assume and hereby disclaims any liability to any party for any loss, damage, or disruption caused by errors or omissions, whether such errors or omissions result from accident, negligence, or any other cause.

Any examples, stories, references or case studies are for illustrative purposes only and should not be interpreted as testimonies and/or examples of what reader and/or consumers can expect. Any statements, strategies, concepts, techniques, exercises and ideas in this information, materials and/or seminar training offered are simply opinion or experience, and thus should not be misinterpreted as promises.

WHAT OTHERS ARE SAYING...

"This powerful, practical book is loaded with proven ideas and strategies you can use to get better results immediately."

—**Brian Tracy,** President Brian Tracy International

"Having known Mark Given for 20 years, I know he lives his philosophy of **TRUST** Bases Leadership, Sales and Success every day. He has shared that knowledge with you in this book."

—**Zan Monroe,** CEO, Author, Speaker and Coach

"My friend, Mark Given has created his life and business based on building **Trust**. Now you have an amazing opportunity to learn his Trust Based Philosophy. Read his book…it can change your life!"

—**Jo Mangum,** Coach, Trainer, Author of *The Strategic Agent*®

"Mark lives his life by the values he shares about **Trust**. This book will not only show you how to build **Trust**, but how to use it and apply the principles in your everyday life. This book is a must read!"

—**Lee Barrett,** Author, Tutor, National Real Estate Instructor, Broker

"I've not only had the privilege of seeing Mark teach but also taught alongside him so I know firsthand that as a teacher and author his message is engaging…genuine …and, impactful! If you have not yet had the "Mark experience" this is a must read."

—**Ed Hatch,** *International* NLP Speaker, Author, Coach – Negotiation Expert

"Having worked with Mark in business and volunteer situations, he has my complete *trust*. His books share discoveries and techniques that are easy to understand and implement immediately."

—**Pat Zaby,** REALTOR® and Highly Respected National Speaker and Teacher

"***Trust*** Mark to create strategies that can be immediately implemented by everyone!"

—**Frank Serio,** Past National President of Council of Residential Specialists

"Mark has provided for us an excellent resource to apply what we know is needful for ***Trust***. I love his list of concepts to make ourselves Trust Based Leaders. The beauty in this book is in asking yourself the questions he provides and adding thoughtful answers to lock the concept into your regular practice of leading."

—**Monica Neubauer,** Speaker, Podcaster

"There are writers and speakers and then there are teachers. My good friend Mark is a teacher. He has captured the essence of the most critical aspect of relationships in a way that made me reflect on my own life and leadership. This short read has long-term impact. Thank you Mark for compiling such profound information on a ***Trust Based Philosophy***."

—**Jackie Leavenworth,** Author, International speaker, trainer and business coach.

CONTENTS

A Message to You! 11

Proven Way #1
Trust Based Leaders Set Priorities 13

Proven Way #2
Trust Based Leaders Exemplify High Integrity 15

Proven Way #3
Trust Based Leaders Show Respect 17

Proven Way #4
Trust Based Leaders Have Vision 19

Proven Way #5
Trust Based Leaders Understand the Power of Why 23

Proven Way #6
Trust Based Leaders Have Focus 25

Proven Way #7
Trust Based Leaders Show Exemplary Qualities 27

Proven Way #8
Trust Based Leaders Inspire 29

Proven Way #9
Trust Based Leaders Build a Powerful Culture 31

Proven Way #10
Trust Based Leaders Develop Clear Strategies 33

Proven Way #11
Trust Based Leaders Focus On Organized
Steps to Improvement 37

Proven Way #12
Trust Based Leaders Lead 39

Proven Way #13
Trust Based Leaders Like 41

Proven Way #14
Trust Based Leaders Love 43

Proven Way #15
Trust Based Leaders Understand Plateaus 47

Proven Way #16
Trust Based Leaders Avoid Regrets 49

Proven Way #17
Trust Based Leaders Listen 51

Proven Way #18
Trust Based Leaders are Empathic 53

Proven Way #19
Trust Based Leaders Have Courage 55

Proven Way #20
Trust Based Leaders Have Faith 57

Proven Way #21
Trust Based Leaders Have Character 59

Proven Way #22
Trust Based Leaders Share the Mantle 63

Proven Way #23
Trust Based Leaders Engage 65

Proven Way #24
Trust Based Leaders are Curious 67

Proven Way #25
Trust Based Leaders Dream 69

Proven Way #26
Trust Based Leaders Understand Virtue 71

Book Bonus 73
Mark Given Interviewed by Jack Canfield 74

One Last Message from Mark 89

About Mark Given 91

DEDICATION

It is with profound admiration, respect and love that I dedicate this book and all that I do personally and professionally to my wonderful wife Janice, our sons Blaine, Chase, Kyle, Taylor, our daughter Kerri, and all our grandchildren. Without them, my life and work would be incomplete and I would not know the joy I have experienced nearly every day for four decades. Through the years, I have learned and grown because of many master teachers and speakers that have inspired me. Some know who they are and some don't, but none the less, I thank each of you. Most recently, I have grown to new levels because of my coach and friend James Malinchak. James.......you ROCK! And, without reservation, I thank my Heavenly Father and his Son, of which I believe, none of the positive I have experienced in my life would have been possible and they have proven over and over that there is nearly nothing impossible, although I still can't dunk a basketball on a 10 ft goal!

MOTIVATE AND INSPIRE OTHERS!

"Share This Book"

Retail $24.95

Special Quantity Discounts

5-20 Books	$21.95
21-99 Books	$18.95
100-499 Books	$15.95
500-999 Books	$10.95
1,000+ Books	$8.95

To Place an Order Contact:
(252) 536-1169
www.MarkGiven.com

THE IDEAL PROFESSIONAL SPEAKER FOR YOUR NEXT EVENT!

Any organization that wants to develop their people to become "extraordinary," needs to hire Mark for a keynote and/or workshop training!

"If you are looking for a speaker, trainer and coach that can empower, inspire, and motivate your group, then you must book my friend Mark Given!"
—**James Malinchak,** Featured on ABC's "Secret Millionaire" Best Selling Author of 20 Books

"We hire Mark to share his Trust Based Philosophy in leadership, sales and success with our 1500 members every year!"
—**Zan Monroe,** CEO Long Leaf Pine Association, Author, Speaker and Coach

"You are simply an event planners dream! I have been involved with contracting hundred's of speakers for various programs over the last 24+ years and I consider an exemplary example of an ideal speaker."
—**Rebecca Fletcher,** Director, GIRE, VP of Education

To Contact or Book Mark to Speak:
(252) 536-1169
www.MarkGiven.com

A MESSAGE TO YOU!

I am Mark Given, an enthusiastic motivational speaker, teacher and Amazon #1 bestselling author that has written several self improvement books and spoken at more than 1000 programs across this planet. You may not know me from my books or seminars, but one thing you should know is that we are both very much alike.

Every day, just like you, I strive to be my best and focus on making a positive difference in this wonderful world.

You want to succeed, help your family, be a good friend, make a secure living and be remembered as someone that can be trusted. Me too!

You already know that building or rebuilding Trust is a top priority for companies looking to sell more products, serve more people and capture their markets.

Trust is a critical link to all good relationships whether personal or professional.

Trust is a primary factor in how people work together effectively, build powerful relationships and listen to one another.

Lack of Trust creates poor productivity and low energy.

So, in this important book, you'll learn how to build Trust in many ways and do it more often.

You'll learn how to lead by example, communicate more openly and take responsible action.

Read this book then share it with a friend. They Trust your opinion.

And, thank-you for taking the time to INVEST IN YOURSELF AND IN YOUR FUTURE!

Building greater and deeper Trust begins now...

What is The Trust Based Leadership Philosophy?

PROVEN WAY #1
TRUST BASED LEADERS SET PRIORITIES

Every leader you've ever known that has accomplished any level of success reached their vision by defining their *priorities*. And the only way you will be truly fulfilled as a leader is when your vision is achieved through knowing that you helped and served. Rewards appeared because you gave of yourself and in at least some small way, you made the world a better place. Your leadership skills, wisdom and ability to lead made a difference and you built all of it with trust. Trust in your idea. Trust in yourself. Trust in those that served with you. Trust that your efforts and accomplishments are the results of setting important priorities and trusting that God, the Universe and people that follow helped you fulfill your *priorities*.

> "The key is not to prioritize what's on your schedule, but to schedule your priorities."
>
> —*Stephen R. Covey*

What are your priorities?

PROVEN WAY #2

TRUST BASED LEADERS EXEMPLIFY HIGH INTEGRITY

Integrity [in-teg-ri-tee]

noun

1. adherence to **moral** and **ethical** principles; soundness of moral **character**; **honesty**.
2. the state of being whole, entire, or undiminished: to preserve the integrity of the empire.
3. a sound, unimpaired, or perfect condition: the integrity of a ship's hull.

You gain leadership integrity by being clear on what you mean and want, by demonstrating consistency in your daily activities. You create leadership integrity by being reliable, by showing those you lead that interdependence is critical to your success, by demonstrating to those that follow you that "we're all in this together".

4. You *establish* leadership integrity by showing respect.
5. You *maintain* leadership integrity by being dependable.
6. You *grow* your leadership integrity by speaking the truth.

> "The supreme quality for leadership is unquestionably *integrity*. Without it, no real success is possible."
> —Dwight D. Eisenhower

How do you demonstrate Leadership Integrity?

PROVEN WAY #3

TRUST BASED LEADERS SHOW RESPECT

With over four decades of research on building and maintaining trust, I have found that strong Trust Based Leaders demonstrate five essential qualities.

1. Respect for others – Respect is more than just a feeling, it's an action. You know it when you see it and it's easy to see when respect is in short supply. Done poorly, the damage to your business or your organization is immeasurable. In reverse, demonstrate respect in abundance and watch your company or organization flourish.

2. Service to others – You've likely heard of and witnessed the quality and results of servant leadership. Put other individuals' needs above your own and miracles happen.

3. Justice to all – No bias allowed here. No favoritism admitted. Justice to all may be difficult to deliver, but it's essential to a winning collaboration. Establish in the minds of those you lead a foundation of justice to all and you'll reduce your turnover, you'll put out less political fires, and you'll find an energy in the rank and file that help you grow. It's worth every effort.

4. Honesty at all cost – great leaders are honest with their employees and staff, their customers and their industry. You'll never build respect without a pattern of open and honest actions.

5. Community – It takes a village…nothing more needs to be said here.

> **"The best way to command respect is to be worthy of it."**
> *—Mark Given*

How do YOU currently show respect and how could you improve?

_____

_____

_____

_____

_____

_____

_____

_____

_____

_____

_____

_____

_____

_____

_____

PROVEN WAY #4
TRUST BASED LEADERS HAVE VISION

In his powerful book *The One Thing You Need to Know*, Marcus Buckingham suggests that leaders clarify the future and managers turn talent into production.

I believe that Trust Based Leaders don't have to be prophets or visionaries, but they do need to **clarify the path**.

Managers then work with people to **clear the path**.

Trust Based Leaders see the direction with a clear vision of what things will look like in years to come. Studies show that in the US, Trust Based Leaders tend to only look 3 to 5 years down the road. In other countries like Japan, Trust Based Leaders visualize 25 to 50, sometimes even 100.

How will Trust Based Leaders ever know when they get where they want to be if they don't have a clear vision for what it will look like when they get there? How do you plan for that?

> **"Your full potential will never surpass your creative vision."**
> *—Mark Given*

Write down a specific date. Visualize your circumstances and success on that future date. What do you see?

I want you to find an innovative way to do things exactly the same way they have been done for the past 5 years

PROVEN WAY #5

TRUST BASED LEADERS UNDERSTAND THE POWER OF WHY

Trust Based leaders learn to ask great questions. In your next interview, try including these powerful questions to help you lead more effectively.

1. If you were in my role today, what are the first three things you would do? (This question allows for the possibility that someone else in your organization also has trust based leadership qualities.)

2. Why would you do that? (You now see the wisdom in their suggestions.)

3. What are the three biggest barriers to our success? (This question often uncovers possibilities you've never envisioned. It shows respect for the associate and often defines the level of community within your organization.)

4. What are our three biggest opportunities? (You don't see what you can't see and you don't know what you don't know. Some associates are growing into Trust Based Leaders right in front of your eyes, but you're so busy that you don't see it. This question helps you grow your vision.)

5. Anything else? (Some people will have no gifts to offer, some didn't know they could, some are afraid to share and some will have more than three. Give them a chance to shine.)

> **"Why chop at the branch of the issue when you can choose to work on the trunk?"**
>
> *—Mark Given*

How will you take the opportunity to ask the "why" question?

_____

_____

_____

_____

_____

_____

_____

_____

_____

_____

_____

_____

_____

PROVEN WAY #6
TRUST BASED LEADERS HAVE FOCUS

Some years ago, I surveyed Trust Based Leaders across the country in an organization of over one million people.

My simple, but not simplistic survey, involved the Trust Based Leaders ability to focus and the things they had learned best when they were focused.

Their answers were powerful and match the needs of Trust Based Leaders in every industry I've ever worked with.

Here are the most common suggestions and wisdom:

1. Don't try to accomplish so many things all at once.
2. Strive for balance in your business and in your personal life. An out of kilter company fails, and an out of kilter life crumbles.
3. Focus on the RIGHT things.
4. Captain the ship. Let your managers be the rudder.
5. Continue positive momentum and quickly squash the hurdles.
6. Keep a close eye on local, national and international trends.
7. Learn from past mistakes.

> **"When you're seeking Trust Based Leadership, focus on controlling your sails, not the wind that drives you."**
> —*Mark Given*

What can you do immediately to become more focused?

_____
_____
_____
_____
_____
_____
_____
_____
_____
_____
_____
_____
_____
_____
_____
_____
_____

PROVEN WAY #7

TRUST BASED LEADERS SHOW EXEMPLARY QUALITIES

What makes a GREAT company or organization?

Here's my list:

1. A needed product or service
2. Growing Trust Based Leaders
3. Engaged people
4. A common goal
5. Paved attention on
   - f. Constant improvement
   - g. Innovation
   - h. Reinvention
   - i. Mastery
   - j. Longevity
   - k. A legacy

> **"The quality of a person's life is in direct proportion to their commitment to excellence, regardless of their chosen field of endeavor."**
> —*Vince Lombardi*

What area of the 5 points listed above can you focus on today to continue building the great company or organization you desire?

_____
_____
_____
_____
_____
_____
_____
_____
_____
_____
_____
_____
_____
_____
_____
_____
_____
_____
_____
_____

PROVEN WAY #8

TRUST BASED LEADERS INSPIRE

There are only two ways to influence human behavior

1. You can manipulate it……or……
2. You can *inspire* it

Trust Based Leadership embraces the ability to *rally people* not for a single event, but for years to come.

Simply put, Trust Based Leaders understand that building a powerful company or organization is like sewing a quilt. Each piece has its own value in creating the whole. Bound together carefully and strategically placed.

> **"Think of your team like a quilt your grandmother made. All the patches placed together become a beautiful and valuable blanket."**
> *—Mark Given*

Starting today, what can you do to build a more beautiful quilt?

PROVEN WAY #9

TRUST BASED LEADERS BUILD A POWERFUL CULTURE

The Apple Organization taught me that an organizations' **_Culture_** is like combining computer hardware and software.

The hardware won't work *efficiently* without the proper software–no matter how good the hardware!

Your company or your organization is just like Apple's, yet your company is more than a brand.

And your brand is more than a logo.

As an example in the corporate world, Disney Institute defines an organizations' culture as:

"The systems of values and beliefs an organization has that drives actions and behaviors and influences relationships."

Trust based organizations begin with a mission statement that describes what's wrong with the world and how they intend to fix it.

They follow a powerful mission statement with a well thought out vision statement that describes what the world will look like after they've finished changing it.

Exceptional Trust Based Leaders don't shoot the messenger, but rather embrace the message and this message can become truly powerful.

> **"Leadership is based on *inspiration*, not domination; on *cooperation*, not intimidation."**
> —*William Arthur Ward*

How can you, as a Trust Based Leader personally improve the quality of your organizations culture?

_____

_____

_____

_____

_____

_____

_____

_____

_____

_____

_____

_____

_____

PROVEN WAY #10
TRUST BASED LEADERS DEVELOP CLEAR STRATEGIES

In Jonathan Haidt's book *The Happiness Hypothesis*, Jon suggests that most people approach their work in one of three ways: A **Job**, a **Career** or a **Calling**.

If you see your work as a **Job**, you do it only for the money, and you look at the clock frequently while dreaming about the weekend ahead, and you probably pursue hobbies.

If you see your work as a **Career**, you have larger goals of advancement, promotion, and prestige. The pursuit of these goals often energizes you, and you sometimes take work home with you because you want to get the job done properly. Yet at times, you wonder why you work so hard. You might occasionally see your work as a rat race.

If you see your work as a **Calling**, you find your work intrinsically fulfilling. You see your work as contributing to the greater good or as playing a role in some larger enterprise the worth of which seems obvious to you. You have frequent experiences of "flow" during the work day, and you neither look forward to "quitting time" nor feel the desire to shout "Thank God it's Friday"! You would continue to work, perhaps even without pay, if you suddenly became very wealthy.

Trust Based Leaders understand the alignment.

When you create systems that do good…..high quality work that produces something of value…these same systems match up with doing well, producing wealth, creating personal and professional advancement…and the world ultimately becomes a better place to live.

Jonathan concludes that "just as plants need sun, water, and good soil to thrive, people need love, work, and a connection to create something larger than themselves.

It's when Trust Based Leaders run their systems right that a sense of purpose and meaning emerge.

> **"We have a strategic plan. It's called doing things."**
> —*Herb Kelleher*

Do you consider YOUR work a **Job**, a **Career**, or a **Calling**?

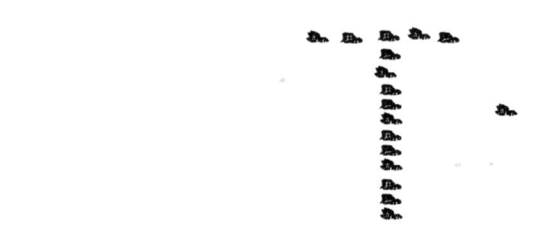

Look, those ducks must really trust their leader.

PROVEN WAY #11

TRUST BASED LEADERS FOCUS ON ORGANIZED STEPS TO IMPROVEMENT

Trust Based Leaders regularly follow the Ritz Carlton pattern to achieve quality improvement.

The US military follows similar patterns.

Each day, Ritz Carlton Ladies and Gentlemen evaluate their personal and professional improvement in six categories.

1. Identify and select a problem area
2. Analyze the problem
3. Generate potential solutions to prevent the same problem from occurring again
4. Select and plan the steps of their chosen solution
5. Implement the solution when the opportunity presents itself again
6. Evaluate the results of their solution

Trust Based Leaders realize that this improvement may appear simple, but it's not simplistic.

Trust Based Leaders realize that what sets them apart from the masses is that most people, companies, and organizations can't compete because they choose to not have formal quality improvement considerations.

> **"Success doesn't come from competing with others, but setting your own *priorities* and *achieving them.*"**
> —*Eddie "The Eagle" Edwards*

What can you do today to improve your service or product?

_____

_____

_____

_____

_____

_____

_____

_____

_____

_____

_____

_____

_____

_____

_____

_____

PROVEN WAY #12
TRUST BASED LEADERS LEAD

Trust Based Leaders develop vision skills rather than just leadership skills. They are proactive rather than reactive.

For the same reasons, you've never seen a dirty fire truck.

Why are fire trucks so clean?

Because when there isn't a fire, the firemen clean their trucks.

The structures of most businesses are designed to put out immediate fires or look for fires.

They function and focus reactively.

Trust Based Leaders are firemen. They work hard to focus on and finish their assignments.

They've been taught to clean their plates and then immediately clean their trucks.

And when they're not fighting fires, they don't go looking for one.

Instead, they clean fire trucks. They show attention to detail which prepares them for growth and success.

What a great way to describe Trust Based Leaders…they sure have clean fire trucks.

> **"Do not go where the path may lead, go instead where there is not path and leave a trail."**
> —*Ralph Waldo Emerson*

What can you do to begin cleaning your fire truck?

_____

_____

_____

_____

_____

_____

_____

_____

_____

_____

_____

_____

_____

_____

_____

PROVEN WAY #13
TRUST BASED LEADERS LIKE

Trust Based Leaders like what they do and they like who they do it with.

They look for the good and they find it…in themselves and in those they associate with.

Trust Based Leaders understand that in an overwhelmingly large number of cases, the likeability factor is given far more weight than the technical factor.

And being a Trust Based Leader is perhaps our most important trigger.

Getting people to do what you want is easy when people like you and trust you, and it helps if you are also considered a friend (or at least that you care enough to become a friend).

> "Be careful the environment you choose for it will shape you; be careful the friends you choose for you will become like them."
> —W. Clement Stone

What can you do to become more likeable?

PROVEN WAY #14
TRUST BASED LEADERS LOVE

Trust Based Leaders know by experience that they will get exactly what they give, but they have to give it first.

Love will return to us many fold, the giving should be a simple act, and your world without will become a reflection of your world within.

Men do not attract that which they want, but rather that which they are.

Trust Based Leaders know that to have more love, they must give more love.

> "There is more hunger for love and appreciation in this world than for bread."
>
> —*Mother Teresa*

How can you show more love to your associates, your family and your friends?

*Yes, thank you for coming
and when we need someone with integrity, we'll keep you in mind!*

PROVEN WAY #15

TRUST BASED LEADERS UNDERSTAND PLATEAUS

Around 1991, George Leonard wrote *Mastery – the Keys to Success and Long-Term Fulfillment*.

In his book, George emphasized that in seeking mastery, we always experience a series of plateaus.

He suggested that to love the plateau is to love what is most essential and enduring in life.

At times, we fail, but then we always level out.

It's during the pause that we would be smart to prepare well for the next acceleration, to plan for and direct our sights towards new levels of success.

Trust Based Leaders know that life and business will never be only an upward charge.

Take advantage of the plateau. Rest, regenerate and prepare.

The next trust is coming*!*

> **"Be kind, for everyone you meet is fighting a hard battle"**
> —*Plato*

When was you last plateau and how well did you handle it?

PROVEN WAY #16

TRUST BASED LEADERS AVOID REGRETS

Bronnie Ware's shares 5 common final regrets in her powerful book, *The Most Common Regrets of the Dying*.

1. I wish I'd lived my life the way I wanted and not the way others expected me too
2. I wish I hadn't worked so hard and enjoyed more of my life
3. I wish I'd had the courage to express my true feelings
4. I wish I'd done a better job of staying in touch with my friends
5. I wish I'd let myself be happier

Trust Based Leaders assist associates to live within a vision of what they really want, their "Why" and not live a life full of regrets.

> **"When one door closes, another opens; but we often look so long and so regretfully upon the closed door that we do not see the one which has opened for us."**
> —*Alexander Graham Bell*

What could you do to eliminate future regrets?

PROVEN WAY #17
TRUST BASED LEADERS LISTEN

Trust Based Leaders know that to become a better listener, they'll need to ask more questions and talk less.

They hear more when they listen.

Maslow would council us to listen "not for whether people are complainers, but rather to what people are complaining about" which distracts them from giving their best.

Some studies show that nearly 70% of organizational errors are attributed to poor communication and slow or no listening skills.

Listening with the heart is a valuable asset.

According to the US Food and Drug Administration, we recall only 17% of what is said to us, but we remember 80% of the emotional message.

There's a very old Chinese Proverb that goes;

"Listen with the intent to hear."

Listen and ask questions, what a simple concept.

How can you begin to listen more with your heart and less with your ears?

_____
_____
_____
_____
_____
_____
_____
_____
_____
_____
_____

> **"Champions aren't made in the gym. Champions are made from something they have deep inside them – a desire, a dream, a vision."**
>
> —*Muhammad Ali*

PROVEN WAY #18

TRUST BASED LEADERS ARE EMPATHIC

Trust Based Leaders know that to be understood is one of the highest human needs.

In the important book *A Whole New Mind*, Daniel Pink writes of a nurse that travels to medical schools teaching "The Craft of Empathy", and cheers the importance of her leadership work.

You'll learn from Daniel the power in the nurses' non-verbal cues like facial expressions, intonation and body language and how these cues help doctors and nurses better grasp what ails their patients.

According to the Gallup organization, nurses consistently rank as the most honest and ethical persons in the US. Isn't that interesting? Therein lies an important lesson.

Trust Based Leaders hone their empathy skills.

"No one gets out of this world alive, so the time to live, learn, care, share, celebrate, and love is now."
—*John Randolph*

Where could you go to learn more about enhancing your skills of empathy?

PROVEN WAY #19

TRUST BASED LEADERS HAVE COURAGE

Trust Based Leaders know it takes courage to see the current reality.

Trust Based Leaders have the courage to dare.

The most effective and successful Trust Based Leaders have two types of courage

1. They have the courage to get startzed and take action
2. They have the courage to endure and the perseverance to not give up

Courage is the single most decisive trait in a Trust Based Leader.

> **"Take chances, make mistakes. That's how you grow. Pain nourishes your courage. You have to fail in order to practice being brave."**
> —*Mary Tyler Moore*

What can you do today to show more courage?

PROVEN WAY #20
TRUST BASED LEADERS HAVE FAITH

Trust Based Leaders know that faith and belief in a positive future leads to powerful actions today.

Trust Based Leaders have the faith of a farmer.

They know that proper cultivating, smart planting, efficient watering, and timely harvesting will fill the grainery.

And Trust Based Leaders understand that answers to their prayers most often don't come when they're waiting, but rather when they're working.

> **"Faith is taking the first step, even when you don't see the whole staircase."**
>
> —*Martin Luther King, Jr.*

How can you show more faith in yourself and those you lead?

PROVEN WAY #21
TRUST BASED LEADERS HAVE CHARACTER

Trust Based Leaders know that competence matters, but character matters more.

I love what Robin Sharma said in his book, *The Monk Who Sold His Ferrari*.

"You sow a thought, you reap an action. Reap an action and sow a habit. Sow a habit and reap a character. Sow a character and reap your destiny."

> **"Though intellect stands high, character stands higher."**
> *—Theodore Roosevelt*

What qualities or character will you be remembered for?

Can you start today? We have the followers YOU deserve

PROVEN WAY #22

TRUST BASED LEADERS SHARE THE MANTLE

It's not about you, it's about them.

The best way to increase your influence is to give it away.

Lead from the heart. The substance of influence is pull not push.

Trust Based Leaders do the work, stay hugely humble, get mud on their boots and trust their replacements.

> "We can't influence until we've been influenced. We can't change others until we ourselves are changed."
> —*Mark Given*

When and how should you begin the process of replacing yourself?

PROVEN WAY #23

TRUST BASED LEADERS ENGAGE

Trust Based Leaders know the statistics that when a manager ignores their workers, the odds of the worker being engaged are 1 in 50.

So, the more you get to know and know about your people the more you can engage and know when to engage with them.

Sometimes, you can make someone's day simply by the way you engage them.

A smile, a kind gesture, a hello at the coffee machine or water cooler can make a real difference to someone that is struggling.

Don't be a tyrant, be a friend (or at least show some semblance that you actually care).

Remember that in both stable and unstable times, growth and improvement are a result of Trust Based Leaders who engage with their organization, instead of managers who constantly focus on pushing their employees to do more with less through pressure and force, know them well enough to know how to encourage them to do more with less.

Quality leadership is achieved through quality contact.

> **"It takes teamwork to make your dream work!"**
> *—James Malinchak*

How can you spend more time engaging your people?

_____

_____

_____

_____

_____

_____

_____

_____

_____

_____

_____

_____

_____

_____

_____

_____

_____

PROVEN WAY #24

TRUST BASED LEADERS ARE CURIOUS

When customers believe you can solve their problems, they are more curious about knowing what you know.

When managers believe you are interested in their success, they are more curious about finding ways to make their jobs more secure so they can advance.

When staff and employees know you listen to their problems, they become curious about how to produce more while being safe and efficient.

Making prospects, managers and employees curious might only take a minute, but those minutes give you an opportunity to establish relationships that improve your bottom line.

"Curiosity is the wick in the candle of learning."
—*William Arthur Ward*

When will you take the time to become more curious?

PROVEN WAY #25

TRUST BASED LEADERS DREAM

As John Maxwell teaches, "Ordinary people can live extraordinary lives when they follow their dreams."

It would always be much better for a Trust Based Leader to do what they love and love what they do…following a dream?

James Allen penned it this way in his powerful little book *As a Man Thinketh*;

"Dream lofty dreams, and as you dream, so shall you become. Your vision is the promise of what you shall one day be; your total ideal is the prophecy of what you shall at last unveil."

"The greatest achievement was at first and for a time a dream. The oak sleeps in the acorn; the bird waits in the egg; and in the highest vision of the soul a waking angel stirs."

> **"Dreams are the seedlings of realities."**
> —*James Allen*

How can you enable the dreams of others?

PROVEN WAY #26

TRUST BASED LEADERS UNDERSTAND VIRTUE

vir·tue–/ v rCHoo/

noun

1. behavior showing *high moral standards*
2. (in traditional Christian angelology) the seventh highest order of the ninefold celestial hierarchy

A few years ago, while at the graduation ceremony for my son Kyle, a brand new dentist, the commencement speaker shared an interesting definition for virtue which I had never considered.

The speaker simply described two kinds of virtue…resume' and eulogy.

Resume' virtues are defined as the skills you bring to the market place. Resume' virtues get you hired.

Eulogy virtues are defined as the way you live your life, the way you are remembered. Eulogy virtues are your legacy, but while living and in death.

Trust Based Leaders understand that real joy, happiness and contentment come from focusing equally on each.

Money alone will not bring you the complete life you seek.

I love what Darren Hardy shared when he said;

> **"The greatest waste in the world is the difference between what we are and what we are capable of becoming."**
> —*Darren Hardy*

As I conclude this book in my Trust Based Philosophy series, I ask you two final important questions;

What can you do to develop more Eulogy virtues?

_____

_____

_____

_____

_____

_____

_____

_____

_____

_____

_____

_____

_____

_____

BOOK BONUS

MARK GIVEN INTERVIEWED BY JACK CANFIELD

Jack Canfield: Hi. I'm Jack Canfield, co-author of the New York Times number one best-selling series, *Chicken Soup for the Soul*, co-author of *The Success Principles*, and a featured teacher in the movie, *The Secret*. I'm sitting here today in an interview with Mark Given. I find Mark to be one of the more interesting and fun people I've ever interacted with, so I'm looking forward to our interview today.

Mark Given: Thank you.

Jack Canfield: Let's start with this, just tell our viewers a little bit about who you are and what you do.

Mark Given: Well, Jack, I've spent nearly 40 years studying the science and the art of building trust. I've written several books on this important subject, directed towards trust based leadership, trust based selling, and trust based success. I travel the country doing mostly keynotes and breakout sessions, half day, or full day sessions, sometimes multi-day sessions on teaching the four steps, or the four stages of trust to companies, and organizations, and associations, and groups that want to succeed by understanding the importance of building trust with their customers and clients, or with their staff, with their employees, with all the people they serve, even their own families.

It's fun. It's exciting. It's interesting to see people when the lights come on and they realize that trust is the foundation of everything. When people lose trust, it's difficult to rebound.

It is so very important that we teach these four stages of trust that are critical to success and are relevant to what all of us do.

Jack Canfield: I'm going to ask you about those four stages in a moment.

Mark Given: Good.

Jack Canfield: But, before I do that. I know you're very passionate about what you do. How did you get into trust being your focus? Why are you so passionate about it?

Mark Given: Well, Jack, there are probably a lot of reasons for that. First of all, when I graduated from college, all I really wanted to do was be in business. So, I went into retail for 20 years and had a pretty successful company in North Carolina, and Virginia. What I discovered was that if my employees didn't trust me, they would steal from me. If customers didn't like us and trust us, they would just do business with somebody else. I eventually sold that company and got into real estate. I discovered it was exactly the same thing with my customers, and clients, and all of the other people I worked with within the real estate industry.

When there's no trust, it's very difficult to succeed.

On top of all that and probably the most important thing personally is that my lovely bride of 40 years and I have five children, and we meant to do that.

I've discovered in life that maintaining trust with your spouse and with your children is critical to happiness and success. It's tough to be successful in any portion of your life when there's no foundation of trust.

I started studying that years ago, not realizing that I was studying the art and the science of trust, but I began by reading books. Books like yours Jack, *Chicken Soup for the Soul*. Many of the stories you included talk about trust, and love, and care and how people feel.

The Success Principles has many of the same principles. There are many other good, really powerful books, that in theory cover the art of building trust.

But I've also discovered that there are no tricks to it. It's just a simple, yet not simplistic science and an art to understanding how to be trustworthy. How you can show people that they can really count on you and care about you and that you care about them.

It's been exciting to spend all these years really studying the art and science of trust and developing some clarity on the 4 Stages of Trust.

Jack Canfield: You know it's funny. I hadn't thought of this in years, but I'm a human potential trainer.

Mark Given: Yes, of course you are.

Jack Canfield: I do workshops and so on. One of the first workshops I ever took was with a guy named Jack Gibb who wrote a book called Trust. He taught this model called TORI. Trust, T-O-R-I, trust leads to openness, openness leads to self-realization and realization of others, and that leads to interdependence and independence instead of co-dependence and dominate dependence.

Mark Given: Sure. That's correct.

Jack Canfield: That's so cool. Thank you for reminding me of one of the major pillars of my own consciousness.

Mark Given: That's terrific. I'm glad I could help just a little.

Jack Canfield: We talked about the 4 Stages of Trust. Talk about that a little bit.

Mark Given: Well, what we've discovered in our own studies is there is nothing else out there similar to what we've done, to individualize these 4 Stages of Trust.

But, there really are 4 stages.

The first stage is ***The Introduction Stage***, or what I call, the ***Grand Opening***.

There are several studies by highly respected Universities now that show people make a decision about you and me in 38 to 55 milliseconds. We've formed the same opinions just as other people form an opinion of us. We decide and they decide whether they like us or can trust us in less than a blink of the eye.

They decide whether they want to associate with us, or do business with us. They decide whether they want to be around us or not be around us that quickly.

And, the Grand Opening is just the 1st critical stage of trust.

The million dollar question then is; *how do we perform at a high enough level so we always have our best Grand Opening ready to deliver to everyone we meet…anytime…anywhere?*

The 2nd Stage of Trust is also very important. We call that the ***Rapport Building Stage***.

Stage 2 is where we get to know people. It's really more about learning to ask good questions and then really listening for the answers. There's an old Chinese proverb that says, "Listen with the intent to hear."

What I've discovered is that when we spend more time asking and then really listening, we become a friend and a confidant.

It is amazing how much we can learn about people and how you build a foundation of trust by just listening and not talking.

Jack Canfield: My wife always says to me, "You want to focus on being more inter-rested than being interesting."

Mark Given: That's right.

Jack Canfield: Exactly.

Mark Given: You go a lot further by being interested.

Jack Canfield: Exactly.

Mark Given: Then, the 3rd Stage of Trust is the ***Maintenance Stage***.

That's where we do all the things that are important to maintain trust. We do that by serving and being more of a giver than a taker.

We all know people that are givers. They are the kind of people we want to associate with.

The 3rd stage is all the skills necessary to become more giving.

Bob Burg and John David Mann wrote a wonderful book that reflects this stage perfectly.

It's called *The Go-Giver*. A very simple, yet powerful book.

Jack Canfield: I know, I've read that.

Mark Given: But this principle is also really profound. I've gotten to know both Bob and John for that reason. It's such an important book. It's being a giver instead of a taker. The world is full of takers.

Then, the 4th Stage of Trust is the one that we all need because sometimes we mess up, no matter how good we are, how smart we are.

It's the **Apology Stage** or what I also call the **Repair Stage**.

This stage is the science and the study of how to apologize. How do you repair the damage once you've made a mistake?

That really relates to companies as well as people. I mean, gosh, how many articles are there every day now, online about some company or individual that has damaged trust with their customers or associates, or the country or the world. It relates to business. It relates to life and it relates to our own personal relationships with the people we care about.

Those are the four important stages, and they're very separate because the skills necessary for each are very different. That's why I spend the time teaching people and speaking to people about how to be their best in each of the four stages.

Jack Canfield: Now I wish I had three hours, I'd literally attack all four of those in-depth. But, I will ask you one follow-up question. You talked about the 1st Stage and the **Grand Opening**, and you only have 55 milliseconds. That's 55 thousandths of a second.

Mark Given: That's right.

Jack Canfield: Which is like, how do you even measure that? But, give us a clue about how you, in that 55 thousandths of a second, what can, or should, someone do?

Mark Given: Well, of course it begins with the way you look. It's your facial expressions. It's the way you dress. Those are the simple things, the obvious things.

But I've discovered a more complex process. It's what we do in our verbal opening.

We've all been taught a standard opening or greeting. We call that a two-step greeting. It's goes……Hi, I'm ……

That introduction is focused on ourselves. It's all about ME.

What I've learned in all these years of research is that when we teach people to go from a two-step greeting to a three-step greeting that it changes the way people feel about us. And the bonus is that we actually listen better. It actually subliminally demonstrates interest in the other person.

As simple as that may sound, it's not simplistic. When we're teaching the **Grand Opening**, we spend some time teaching people to go from a two-step greeting to a three-step greeting, which opens up a whole new realm of trust. And the magic is that we do it in just the very first few seconds of meeting someone new.

It can also be used with people we already know well. As is said in some circles, the 3 Step Opening is a game changer.

Jack Canfield: What are those three-steps?

Mark Given: The three-steps are simple. You go from, it's all about me to it's really about you. And I mean that literally.

In other words, instead of saying, "Hi, I'm me." You would say, "Hi, it's good to see YOU (or something similar). I appreciate the opportunity for us to be here, Jack. Thank YOU for doing this. Then, I'd share my name."

We would actually use the word, YOU twice, instead of making it quickly about yourself.

Jack Canfield: Yeah, I hear that.

Mark Given: Instead of hey, or hi, or hello, I'm me. It's hello. It's good to see YOU. Thank YOU for interviewing me. Boy, sure appreciate YOUR time today.

When I get done with the three-steps, or the initial two-steps, then I get to the "I'm Mark Given."

But, what we've also found as a bonus is that when people go from a two-step greeting to a three-step greeting, they more often walk away and actually remember the name of the person that they just were introduced to.

Jack Canfield: Interesting.

Mark Given: Often, when you use the two-step greeting, you walk away and you forget. Now, what was her name again? We take memory courses and try to do all these things, and just going from a two-step greeting to a three-step greeting is a remarkable change in the science of trust, building trust and creating an immediate likeable bound.

Jack Canfield: That's fascinating. I'd love to interview you about all this. I'll have to take your course! And I can tell that you are passionate about this.

Mark Given: I am.

Jack Canfield: You've talked about why you're so passionate about it. There are a lot of people talking about trust. I know Stephen M.R. Covey and others. What makes your work different?

Mark Given: Well, what we've learned is there's really not a single person, there's not a company, or an association, or organization out there that has not benefited from our programs and teaching steps. Instead of just a concept of building trust, we actually teach people how to do it.

Jack Canfield: How to do it and it is needed.

Mark Given: And we teach the steps on how to do it. We do it in those different formats, in a keynote, or breakout, or a half for full-day session, so that we can actually delve into those 4 different Stages of Trust and teach them the techniques. There are a lot of motivational speakers out there, and certainly, we motivate, but the difference, I feel, and what makes me so passionate about this is, when I'm out speaking and I see the lights come on in their brain and they think, "Oh, I could use that. How did I not know that, or how did I miss that, or gosh, I just made that mistake, or I said something or I did something and here's how I fix it."

It's really exciting to get those emails, or a note, or something from somebody that says, "Thanks for teaching me that. Thanks for helping. Here's what happened as a result. I went home and did this, or I had a customer or client, my best client, that I really messed it up and I've been able to repair that because of these important techniques."

It's exciting to get up in the morning and get out and do what I do, because this changes lives. It changes businesses.

Jack Canfield: You know, it's so sad that our schools don't teach these skills.

Mark Given: Sure. I agree.

Jack Canfield: I always tell people, "Tell me the five causes of the civil war." No one can even remember them, but we study that for days, or weeks. But, we're not learning communication skills, relationship skills, self-management skills.

It's like we have to go into the hotels and the conference centers to learn what's really important. You're out there doing that. That's great. When you look at the clients you have, are there common challenges that people are facing out there in relation to this? How do you help them address those?

Mark Given: Yes, Jack. What I've found is that we all make mistakes. We all want the same thing and that's to build trust with people. People that we care about, or people we want to associate with, or people we want to do business with.

The real challenge is that we all experience much of the same thing. We have good days and we have bad days. When we have those bad days, we need some methods to improve and to repair. Just look at the statistics on marriages these days and you can see that clearly, there's a need for what I do and have studied. Although, I spend the majority of my time in the business world, the relationship world, marital world, could also use the techniques and skills too.

It's really exciting and fun to get out and help people see that they can do it. It's not about what I've learned, or sharing some things, it's what they can actually go and apply immediately themselves.

Jack Canfield: I'm sure you find too, like from my work, if I do a corporate training, the people take those same skills home with their wife, with their neighbors, in their church, with their children.

Mark Given: Sure, absolutely.

Jack Canfield: Absolutely, very good. If someone's sitting out there watching this, they're probably thinking, "Yeah, I don't know all that stuff about phases of trust and how to do it and I've lost some business because of, perhaps, betraying a trust, or not knowing how to build that rapport and trust." They're thinking about, perhaps, hiring you to work with them. What would you tell them?

Mark Given: I'd say, "Please, give me a call."

Jack Canfield: Plain and simple.

Mark Given: Please give me a call, because I'm pretty confident that there's something, whether you're a leader and trying to build trust with your organization, your staff, or your employees, or whether you're a sales person trying to build trust with your clients or customers, or you're just trying to build a successful life.

What I would say is that we have some things that can help you. That, given even just a little bit of time, we can share important trust building systems that people can apply immediately. So they can go home or back to work and actually do something.

What's fun is to see people actually go home and do something. So, call me, they can reach me at MarkGiven.com. It's really easy to find me and I invite anyone that could benefit to do that.

Jack Canfield: You're not in the witness protection program.

Mark Given: I'm not, thank goodness, you can find me.

Jack Canfield: Very good, very good. Well, Mark, this is fascinating. I think trust is critical … It's a foundational thing, that everything else is built on. If you don't have it, nothing moves forward. Thanks for being my guest today. I really appreciate it.

Mark Given: My pleasure Jack, absolutely my pleasure.

Jack Canfield: If you want to build more trust in your relationships, in your organization, if you want to teach your people, whether they're sales people, managers, whatever it might be, at your association meeting, or convention, your conference, an in-house workshop, whatever, Mark Given can help you do that. Check out his website at MarkGiven.com.

TRUST BASED
PHILOSOPHY

ONE LAST MESSAGE FROM MARK

Thank-you!

My good friend Zan Monroe once say, "*what you focus on expands*" and I have witnessed that to be true over and over in the life of others and in my own life.

In brief definition, Zan meant that the things you concentrate your time and talents on become the things that are not only most important to you but become what you are often known and respected for.

Trust is one of those things I want to be known and respected for and I believe it either is or should be for you too.

Why?

Because, when the people you love the most really and deeply trust you, your life is filled with joy. When your friends trust you, your life becomes fun. When the people you lead trust you, things get accomplished and when your clients and customers trust you, you create financial security and wealth.

So, thank-you for taking your valuable time to invest in you by reading this book…but reading is just the first step.

Now, you have to go out and actually apply it every day.

You can do it though, and the time to start is now!

I'm just one of the people rooting for your success, so go get a piece of paper right now and write down where and how you're going to begin building more Trust.

Then, when it's convenient, drop me a note or an email and let me know how it all worked out for you.......YOUR success story. I always love hearing success stories and with your permission, it might just make my next book!

You can reach me at:

Mark Given International
P.O. Box 1460
Roanoke Rapids, NC 27870
mark@markgiven.com

ABOUT MARK GIVEN
Founder of the Trust Based Philosophy

The Speaker
Mark has been changing businesses and improving lives for nearly four decades. He has shared Leadership Training, Sales Mastery and Trust Based Philosophy systems with thousands of people just like you and has worked with hundreds of businesses across the world. His audiences say that Mark's speaking and teaching delivery is timely, relevant, witty, engaging, funny, cutting edge and a breath of fresh air.

The Author
In addition to his speaking and teaching career, Mark is a prolific author; evidenced by his Trust Based Philosophy book series and his Amazon #1 Best Selling book "Finding My Why Ernie's Journey". Mark has also co-written three additional books and writes his weekly blog "Mark's Minute" which is read by people all over the world every week. Mark continues to have a powerful influence through his keynote speeches, educational sessions, books, and recordings. Mark knows and loves to share the skills, language, and stories of accomplished business leaders from diverse industries (sales, real estate, banking, insurance, education, service, and many others). He understands how to identify the practical and simple lessons that grow people, their businesses and their lives.

The Person
Mark grew up in a rural Ohio town, headed to North Carolina to finish college, and resides in a small NC community with his wonderful wife Janice. Together, they have raised 5 great kids and strive to inspire all their grandchildren. Mark and Janice's

four sons are all Eagle Scouts and Entrepreneurs and their daughter is the apple of Mark's eye.

The Businessman

After his education at The Ohio State University and Elon College, Mark spent 20 years as CEO of a multi-state retail sales and rental company that grew to 47 locations. The next years have included international speaker/teacher, REALTOR©, volunteer, and community leader. All along the way, Mark has invested tens of thousands of hours speaking and teaching his life and business changing Trust Based Philosophy systems, leadership skills, sales skills and personal mastery systems with companies and organizations just like yours.

TRUST BASED
PHILOSOPHY

Mark Given International
www.markgiven.com
252-536-1169
mark@markgiven.com